Sa...ey

Trail

and other walks around the village of Sawley in Derbyshire

by Geoffrey Kingscott

Published by the
Sawley and District Historical Society
2009

www.sawleyhistoricalsociety.org.uk

ISBN 978-0-9552878-1-7

Publication was made possible thanks
to the generous support of the
Sawley Parish Council

Thanks are due to Pam Mee who drew the
maps; to Laurence Kingscott, who tested the
walks; to Judy Kingscott who edited the text,
and to various members of the society who
contributed suggestions.

Cover photograph: Sawley Church by the river Trent

Printed by Glenwood Printing, Unit 4, Baines
Industrial Park, Woods Lane, Derby DE22 3UD

The Sawley Trail

The walk covers approximately one and a half miles along pavements and is suitable for wheelchairs. Bold numbers in brackets in the text correspond with those on the map which you will find on the back cover.

The village of Sawley lies in the south-east corner of Derbyshire, on the northern bank of the River Trent. Free car parking can be found next to the Sawley Community Centre on Draycott Road, Sawley, NG10 3FR, Ordnance Survey grid reference SK 473318. This is the location we have chosen for the start of the Trail.

Long Eaton Railway Station (which, incidentally, was originally called Sawley Junction – its name was changed in 1968) is one mile from the centre of Old Sawley. Trent Barton's bus service 15 passes the station and also stops at the Community Centre.

Sawley Community Centre [1]

The Sawley Community Centre and Memorial Hall was opened in 1958 as a practical memorial to those from Sawley who lost their lives in the two world wars. The opening ceremony was performed by film star Richard Attenborough, whose maternal grandfather, Samuel Clegg, a notable local personality, lived in Sawley. Behind the Community Centre are playing fields maintained by the Erewash Borough Council.

Before Sawley was incorporated into the Long Eaton Urban District in 1935, the road you are standing on was known as Derby Road; the name was changed to Draycott Road to avoid confusion with another Derby Road in Long Eaton.

RICHARD ATTEN BOROUGH AND HIS WIFE SHEILA
SIM, SEATED CENTRE, LISTENING TO THE SPEECHES
BEFORE THEY OPENED THE SAWLEY COMMUNITY
HALL IN 1958

Draycott Road is close to the alignment of a Roman
road which ran from an important fort at Little Chester,
north of Derby, to the River Trent.

*Walk the few yards to the front of the Co-operative
Society shop.* **[2]**

Just past the shop you will see a pathway, now
blocked by garden extensions. This was once part of
an important footpath which divided close to the
railway line, one branch going across fields to
Wilsthorpe, the other going to Long Eaton.

*Continue along Draycott Road to the corner of
Grosvenor Avenue.*

Opposite you is the Old Sawley Post Office **[3]**. This
used to be a baker's shop, the bread being baked in
the buildings at the back.

The last part of Draycott Road ahead of you, through
to the main road, was only a footpath until after the

second world war. For some years after it had been made into a road it retained a red colour, having been constructed from brick hardcore taken from wartime street air-raid shelters when they were demolished.

Cross Draycott Road and walk down Towle Street, turn right into Arnold Avenue, and stop a few feet short of the Chinese take-away. **[4]**

The single-storey building opposite, standing in its own grounds, is the Sawley Women's Institute. **[5]** It dates from the 1930s and is still in regular use. Behind it is where the air raid siren was sited on a tall pole during the second world war. Beyond you can see the gable end of the former Sawley School.

THE GABLE END OF THE OLD SAWLEY SCHOOL CAN STILL BE SEEN.

Cross the road and walk past the front of the Women's Institute to the car showroom. This building, now somewhat altered, was until the 1950s, the Old Sawley School. **[6]**

SAWLEY SCHOOL WHEN IT WAS STILL USED FOR
EDUCATION.

*Walk towards the main road, and stop in front of the
Nag's Head public house.*

Sawley Market Place [7]
The main road, now known as Tamworth Road, has
been a highway since time immemorial, and in stagecoach days it was 'improved' to become the Lenton
(Nottingham) to Sawley turnpike.

You will notice that Wilne Road, the road you have
walked down, is wider than is justified for a mere side
road. This is because here was once Sawley Market
Place. Sawley, then the most important village for
miles around, was granted township status in a
charter of Henry III in 1259. This authorised it to hold
a weekly market and an annual fair, both now
discontinued.

Where the traffic refuge now stands there used to be
a lamp standard, always known as Big Lamp, and
which itself succeeded a market cross. Wilne Road
used to be known as Cross Street.

Behind you is the Nag's Head, one of Sawley's oldest public houses. The wall on the left-hand side of the Nag's Head shows evidence of the former three-storey Manor (or Market) House which stood here until the middle of the 20th century. The building on the corner opposite was until recently the oldest of Sawley's general shops before being converted into private residences.

SAWLEY MARKET PLACE, 100 YEARS AGO, WITH THE FORMER SHOP ON THE LEFT, 'BIG LAMP', AND THE MANOR HOUSE ON THE RIGHT,

Turn left into Tamworth Road, and walk along to the corner of Fairfield Crescent. **[8]**

Chantry Close, which you have just passed, now set out as old persons' bungalows, includes the former site of Gaol Yard. This used to hold the village lock-up, where miscreants were held before being taken to court in Derby.

The part of Fairfield Crescent which you see in front of you used to be called East End. As this name suggests, it at one time marked the limit of the old village.

EAST END AROUND 1900

Later, as development took place beyond East End, a differentiation was made – which lasts till this day – between Old Sawley and New Sawley. Our walk today is confined to Old Sawley.

Fairfield Crescent, now a private housing estate, was built on a field where in its last days, the annual village wakes, or funfair, were held, hence the name. Formerly the wakes had been held in the streets around the Market Place.

SAWLEY WAKES, WHEN THEY WERE HELD ON THE FAIRFIELD

The older (Victorian) house in Fairfield Crescent which you can see as you enter the crescent was Firs Farm, once one of several farmhouses in the village, but now a private residence. Another, older, building on the right has been altered from what were two cottages, possibly dating from the 18th century. These may have been attached to Ivy Farm, as Ivy Farmhouse (long since demolished) was nearby.

Retrace your steps to the Nag's Head, pass over Wilne Road, then cross Tamworth Road via the refuge outside the White Lion, another of Sawley's old public houses, and proceed to the church.

Sawley Parish Church [9]

The Parish Church of All Saints is obviously one of the glories of Sawley, approached by a magnificent avenue of lime trees, planted in the 1840s. There has been a church on this site since Saxon times.

The oldest extant stonework (probably 11th century but pre-Conquest) is incorporated into the chancel wall, and may have been the external wall of an earlier building. The present nave and aisles in Early English style were built in the 13th century.

The tower and spire are from the 15th century, as are the battlements and the present roof, while the fine clock was installed around 1880. The tower contains a full peal of eight bells, the tenor bell of 1591 being a thanksgiving for the defeat of the Armada.

The interior of the church includes some fine medieval tombs, including several of the Bothe family, and some attractive carved woodwork, including the choir stalls and a Jacobean pulpit.

A DRAWING OF SAWLEY CHURCH MADE IN 1852.
IT HAS CHANGED LITTLE SINCE THEN

Return to the road.

Facing the church gate is a residential development
called Wren Court. This is on the site of what used to
be the Carter's mineral water factory, once a major
Sawley industry. This factory had begun in a small
way at the end of the 19th century, and gradually
expanded, taking over cottages, a bakery, and
Bates's farm in Wilne Road, until it got so big it had to
move to a greenfield site in Leicestershire. The size of
the Wren Court estate shows how much of the centre
of Sawley was once taken up by the factory, which
was a major Sawley employer.

10

THE MAIN ROAD (NOW TAMWORTH ROAD)
100 YEARS AGO. THE COTTAGES ON THE RIGHT
WERE DEMOLISHED WHEN THE ROAD WAS
IMPROVED IN THE 1920s

From the church re-cross Tamworth Road by the same refuge you used before, and then continue left further along Tamworth road, round the corner, past the Harrington Arms, and the last houses of the village, as far as the bridge. Stop at the widest point before the pavement narrows.

Harrington Bridge [10]

The River Trent runs across much of England, from west to east, and is traditionally the boundary between northern England and southern England. Sawley is at the mid-point of its course from its source on Biddulph Moor in Staffordshire to where it flows out into the Humber estuary. It has even been claimed that because of these facts Sawley is the real centre of England!

11

Sawley village was built on rising ground above the shallows of the Trent, where (at least in summer when the water was low), it was at one time possible to cross the river on foot. This ceased to be the case when the river was made navigable at the end of the 18th century.

FIRST BRIDGE OVER THE TRENT AT SAWLEY

The first bridge over the river at this point was built in 1790, paid for by public subscription. The place where you are standing was the site of one of the old toll buildings, which were each side of the road. It is believed that the toll keeper had his living rooms on the downstream side and the bedrooms on the up-stream side. The buildings were demolished in the 1930s.

TOLLHOUSES ON HARRINGTON BRIDGE AT SAWLEY

In no section of the navigable River Trent is there as big a drop in water levels as in the Sawley area. The fall in level is achieved by two major weirs, one just out of sight round the bend of the river to the right, the other a mile down stream, below the power station whose cooling towers are visible in the distance.

To avoid the two weirs the river navigation authority made two short canals, called cuts, the Sawley Cut which though hidden is in front of you, on the other side of the river, and the Cranfleet Cut at Trent Lock. The island formed by the river and Sawley Cut is known as Trent Meadows, and is due to be developed by the river authorities as a nature reserve and recreation centre.

Although much of Sawley has often been affected by flooding from the river, this does not apply to the higher ground on which the church and much of the original village stand, an indication of how good an eye for ground our remote ancestors had.

EARLY FLOODS AT SAWLEY SHOWING HOW THE CHURCH WAS BUILT ON HIGH GROUND JUST ABOVE FLOOD LEVEL

If you turn from the river and look towards the church you may be able to make out the higher ground, though recent flood prevention work has made the distinction less clear.

Between you and the church is the Church Farm housing development. Until recently Church Farm was operating and owned by the Grammer family, Sawley's leading farming family in the 20th century.

Go back towards the village and proceed as far as the car park of the Harrington Arms. As you walk back you pass a wooden gate, now unused and overgrown (likely to affected by bridge improvements in 2009).

This gate gave access for villagers to collect riverbed gravel to repair local roads. It was also the way to the ferry before the bridge was built.

The ferry, which left from a point near the wooden bungalows you can see from the Harrington Arms car park, was discontinued when the bridge was built. The ferryman's cottage has been incorporated into a much larger house.

Harrington Arms [11]

A SKETCH OF THE HARRINGTON ARMS AND NEARBY BUILDINGS, AS THEY APPEARED IN 1850, MADE IN 1912 BY RUSSELL GRAMMER

14

The Harrington Arms public house was an old coaching inn. In stagecoach days passengers disembarked at the Harrington in order to take the ferry. After the bridge was built it served as a place where the horses were changed.

The arms displayed are those of the Earls of Harrington, formerly Lords of the Manor of Sawley.

MOUNTING STEPS IN THE CAR PARK OF THE HARRINGTON ARMS

In the car park of the public house can be seen a flight of steps next to the side entrance to the pub extension. These were mounting steps, now pebble-dashed, used by riders to get on to their horses.

Looking across the fields you will see a track leading to the wooden bungalows used as weekend retreats. Beyond them is a wood of willow trees. This wood is known locally as Willow Root. Willows have always been present in Sawley, which gets its name from one variety, the sallow willow. Basket-making using willow was at one time an important cottage industry in Sawley

To the right of Willow Root, and difficult of access, is the Old Trent, a section of the river now cut off from the main stream. This is a classic example of what geographers call an *oxbow lake*. This phenomenon occurs when a river in spate floods across the open neck of a horseshoe-shaped bend and then adopts this as its new course; the horseshoe is then gradually cut off.

If you look carefully at the field itself you will see the ridges and furrows created when the medieval open field system of strip farming was operated in Sawley.

RIDGE AND FURROW IN THE FIELD BEHIND THE
HARRINGTON ARMS AFTER FLOODING

Return to the main road and continue the short distance to the gates in front of Bothe Hall.

The White House restaurant and hotel you have just passed used to be a general shop operated by the Sawley Co-operative Society until that Society was taken over by the rival one in Long Eaton. The 90 degree bend in the road outside the shop has been there since recorded time.

Bothe Hall
Bothe Hall stands on the site of the residence of the Bothe family, a family closely associated with Sawley and with the Church. In the 15th century it produced eminent churchmen, whose tombs can be seen in the parish church.

16

Bothe Hall now serves as the offices of a computer company.

BOTHE HALL

Running alongside Bothe Hall is Wilne Avenue **[12]**, one of Sawley's *twitchells* or alleyways. The word *twitchell* seems to be peculiar to this part of the world. The further end of this twitchell, past Bothe Hall Meadow, has some interesting old brickwork which we will pass shortly.

*Take this twitchell and follow it to the grassed area where there is pedestrian access to Wren Court **[13]**. Look over the wall into the Baptist Churchyard.*

Samuel Clegg grave [13]

The grave with the upright unshaped stone is that of Samuel Clegg.

He was a leading figure in the history of both Sawley and Long Eaton.

Samuel Clegg was chairman of Sawley Parish
Council, and the first headmaster of the Long Eaton
Secondary School (later Long Eaton Grammar
School). His daughter Mary married a teacher at the
school, Frederick Attenborough, who later became
principal of Leicester University College. Richard
Attenborough the film actor and director, and David
Attenborough the television presenter, are the
children of Mary and Frederick and the grandsons of
Samuel Clegg.

Samuel's son became Sir Alec Clegg, a leading
educationalist, and Alec's son Peter Clegg is today
one of the Britain's leading architects.

*Continue along the twitchell to Wilne Road. Turn right,
and stop outside the Baptist Church.*

Baptist Church [14]

Set back from
Wilne Road in its
own graveyard,
the Baptist Church
is an elegant
building dating
from 1800.

It was extended in
1843 when the
schoolrooms and a
schoolmaster's
house were
added. Samuel
Clegg's father,
Alexander Clegg,
was the
headmaster of the

Baptist School. The Sawley Baptist Church is one of the oldest-established nonconformist organisations in the area, thought to have been formed in 1766.

The Baptist School did not have its own playground so the children had to play out in the street. This street was also used by cows passing to and fro for milking at several nearby farms. The resulting droppings gave the village a bad smell which became known as the "Sawley hum".

Continue along Wilne Road for 75 yards, until you arrive at the entrance to another twitchell, which a sign identifies as Church Avenue.

Dr Clifford's birthplace [15]
The left-hand section of the house with the steep gable was the birthplace of the Rev. John Clifford, and this is commemorated by a plaque.

Dr Clifford (1836-1923) was one of the leading figures in the history of the English Baptist movement, and in his prime exerted considerable political influence. He was a strong supporter of Mr Gladstone, an opponent of the Boer War, and a fierce critic of the 1902 Education Act (because of state support for some Church of England schools). His decision in 1918 to switch his support from the Liberal Party to the Labour Party provided a big electoral boost to Labour.

Continue on Wilne road a few yards round the corner.

If you look up at the older house after the corner you will see a Shipstone's plaque and a metal arm which once held a sign, a reminder of when this building, now a private residence, was yet another of Sawley's public houses (the 'New Inn').

Turn back and cross Wilne Road to the Railway Inn.

Railway Inn [17]
The Railway Inn is not adjacent to any railway line. The reason for its name is that it was on the route out of the village to where Sawley Railway Station used to stand, a mile away at Sawley Lane, Breaston. This station opened in 1839 and closed in 1930. Another railway station, Sawley Junction, opened in 1888 on Tamworth Road in New Sawley, and this is the one still operating today, though now called Long Eaton.

THE RAILWAY INN CIRCA 1940.
NOTE THE CAST-IRON ROAD SIGNS

The house next to the Railway Inn was the site of Sawley's last thatched-roof building, but this was replaced by the present construction in the mid-20th century.

SAWLEY'S LAST THATCHED HOUSE ON WILNE ROAD
IN THE EARLY 20TH CENTURY

*Proceed up Plant Lane to rejoin your starting point at
the Sawley Community Centre and end the trail.*

In Plant Lane you will see, on the right, some
buildings now turned into private residences.

These were once Wright's shoe shop and factory, a
business which served Sawley for 200 years, closing
only in 1979. The Wrights are still an important
Sawley family.

Now you have completed the Sawley Trail, you might
like to try some of the following walks around the
village.

Other walks in or near Sawley
(see map on inside back cover)

TRENT LOCK

This walk to our local beauty spot is approximately four miles across fields, towpaths and footpaths. Sadly it is not suitable for wheelchair users but there is an alternative direct road route to Trent Lock by way of Lock Lane.

Start at the gates to the parish church. With the church at your back, turn right and walk along Tamworth Road in the direction of Long Eaton. You pass the former rectory and another house identified as 'The Old Post Office', then a large field (known in Sawley as Manor Yard).

The two parallel rows of humps and hollows at the far side of this field have been identified as medieval fishponds, possibly belonging to a monastic house on the Church Farm site.

Immediately after passing a group of houses lower than the road level, turn right at the Public Footpath sign and go through a gate to enter the field beside the sub-station. Walk diagonally across to the far end of the field, and climb to the top of the flood bank. Take a few steps to the right until you are level with a white post marking the line of a gas pipe.

If you look back at the field you have just come through, straight ahead of you are a number of humps. These humps are the remains of the oldest known construction in Sawley, a camp which may have been built by Roman auxiliary soldiers. It is more visible in aerial photographs, where it clearly has the playing card shape of a traditional Roman camp.

AERIAL PICTURE OF THE 'ROMAN CAMP', WITH FISHPONDS DIRECTLY ABOVE IN THE FIELD NEARER THE ROAD.

If it was Roman it was probably only a "marching camp" (one set up temporarily when troops were on the march) since there is no archaeological trace of the debris which would be produced by a more permanently occupied site.

The River Trent has always been very prone to flooding, and after Sawley was seriously inundated in 1946 and 1947 a series of floodbanks, such as the one you are now standing on, was erected to protect the residential areas. At the time of writing (2009) all of Sawley's floodbanks are being raised following several years of dangerously high river levels.

The eastbound footpath here (an alternative route to the one set out below) goes under the railway and diagonally across a golf course to reach the flood bank alongside the River Trent.

Your view here will also take in the railway viaduct over the Trent flood plain, and the cooling towers of the Ratcliffe Power Station, looming up over Red Hill.

Continue on the westbound footpath which goes past the back of the churchyard and the former Church Farm, now a residential development. Join the main road at a stile. Cross the road with care, and start walking towards the bridge.

When the pavement narrows, cross back across the main road. Having to cross the main road twice because of the illogicality of lack of pavement on first one side of the bridge and then the other, is an annoyance from which generations of Sawley people have suffered.

After crossing the River Trent, turn left through a gate to access the towpath of the Sawley Cut, and walk in an easterly direction along this towpath.

On your right, on the other side of the Cut, you will see the canal inlet and buildings of the complex known as Sawley Marina. This is one of the largest inland marinas in England. For anyone interested in boats for inland waterways, it is worth a visit in its own right. There is a restaurant and a chandlery.

A SECTION OF THE BOAT SALES AREA AT SAWLEY MARINA

Your towpath walk will bring you, at the end of the Cut, to Sawley Lock, one of the busiest locks in the Midlands. Its attractive lock cottage probably dates back to 1793, when the Cut was made.

SAWLEY LOCK COTTAGE

Cross back to the north bank of the River Trent by the footbridge adjacent to the railway bridge, then turn right beneath a small arch of the bridge. Part of the Trent Lock golf course is on your left.

OLD PHOTO OF A STEAM TRAIN APPROACHING THE BRIDGE OVER THE RIVER TRENT WHEN THIS WAS STILL A PASSENGER LINE.

The railway is these days used almost exclusively for freight, except when the Nottingham to Derby direct line is blocked for some reason.

After walking round the long sweep of a shallow bend in the river, and passing through two gates, you reach the beginning of the area, known as Trent Lock, devoted to leisure activities. These begin with a small caravan site on your left. On the opposite side of the river is a sailing club hut used by the Sea Scouts.

Continue along the riverbank, passing (or stopping for a drink at) the Navigation Inn, one of Trent Lock's two public houses, this one fronted by its large grassed picnic area.

Continue beside the river, and then cross the mouth of the Erewash Canal by a footbridge. Pause in the centre of the footbridge, to admire the scene.

Looking towards the river you will see the handsome white wooden building of the Trent Valley Sailing Club, erected in 1907. Beyond that the Trent makes a sharp left turn, with, just out of sight, a dangerous weir. You can just see the floating safety barrier of orange cylinders. To enable boats to avoid the weir, the Cranfleet Cut was created, and this can be seen to your left. The sailing club is thus on an island formed by the river and the cut.

Rising beyond the river is the ridge known as Red Hill, and coming in from the right, at the bottom of the ridge, is the River Soar, which is navigable, with cuts to avoid the shallow stretches, all the way to Leicester. The confluence of the Soar and the Trent marks the point at which the three Midland counties, Derbyshire, Nottinghamshire and Leicestershire meet.

The railway line to Leicester and London crosses the Trent here and enters the tunnel through Red Hill via unusual castellated portals.

The bridge on which you are standing is over the mouth of the Erewash Canal, constructed to bring coal down from the Erewash Valley coalfields 12 miles away, mainly to supply Leicester via the Soar Navigation. The canal runs at a level higher than the river, so its lock is kept busy lowering and raising boats. This is the actual Trent Lock which eventually gave its name to this small community.

AN EARLY PICTURE OF TRENT LOCK

Until the railway arrived in the mid 19th century taking away most of the canal traffic, special ferry boats were used to take the horses which towed the canal boats, across the Trent to the Soar.

HORSE FERRY LEAVING THE RAMP NEAR THE NAVIGATION INN, WITH NARROW-BOATS MOORED BEHIND

Close to this delightful spot refreshments can be taken either at the Lock House Tea Rooms or at the Steamboat Inn, the second of Trent Lock's public houses.

Continue your walk left along the towpath of the Erewash Canal, past the tearooms and Steamboat, until you come to a high footbridge. You will pass a number of attractive narrowboats and houseboats (one a 'double-decker') which are permanently moored here. Next is Mills Dockyard, a family firm for over a century, where boats are built and restored.

Climb the rather steep steps on the bridge to cross the canal, and follow the short footpath round to join the road known as Lock Lane. Take the footpath on the right-hand side of the road, opposite the Trent Lock Golf Club, which takes you to the railway level crossing. Continue forward to Tamworth Road, and turn left, by Sawley's attractive war memorial, to return to your starting place by the Church.

SHARDLOW AND WILNE

A walk of about six miles along towpaths and field paths, with several stiles. Suitable for dog-walkers, not suitable for either wheelchairs or pushchairs.

From the parish church, walk towards the River Trent, cross the Harrington bridge over the river and the Sawley Cut. Turn right to follow the towpath on the far (Leicestershire) side of the Sawley Cut.

After the Cut ends you can see the safety barrier which prevents boats accidentally going over the weir. You can often hear the sound of the water tumbling over it.

On reaching the bridge which takes the M1 motorway over the river, you will see on your left a large pond of stagnant water. This is known locally as the Hully Gully, representing a former course of the river.

The River Trent has frequently changed its course over the centuries. Just before the impressive cast-iron bridge carrying water pipes, you pass over a broad stream by a footbridge. This stream represents yet another former course of the river.

FOOTBRIDGE OVER AN OLD COURSE OF THE RIVER TRENT

Where the River Trent takes a sharp bend to the left you will see the start of the Trent & Mersey Canal opposite you, and the mouth of the River Derwent to your right. There used to be a bridge here, known as the "long horse bridge", which took the horses pulling narrowboats over to the canal towpath. Plans have been agreed for a new multi-user bridge; by 2009 no date had been fixed for the replacement to be undertaken.

SAWLEY HISTORICAL SOCIETY MEMBERS ON THE
FORMER LONG HORSE BRIDGE BEFORE IT WAS
DEMOLISHED IN 2002

Turn left and follow the track for ¾ mile to a way-marker post.

If you look carefully in the bushes at a field boundary, you will see the discarded remains of a pair of clapper gates almost hidden in the undergrowth. These were the type of gates favoured by the Trent river authorities as they were self-closing, but by the same token, they were difficult for one person to open!

CLAPPER GATES ON THE RIVER TRENT BEFORE
THEY WERE DISMANTLED

At the Waymarker post leave the track and follow the footpath which keeps close to the river. When you reach farm buildings follow the path round by a wall to a stile into a side road. Continue to the main Shardlow road. Cross the river by the modern road bridge.

30

On the opposite side of the road is an interesting piece of stonework showing the tolls which used to be levied on those using the bridge over the Trent. The present bridge is a replacement for the ancient bridge, which was destroyed by floods in 1947.

In the 18th century Shardlow was a major inland port, as its many attractive warehouses and Georgian homes indicate.

Walk as far as the bridge over the Trent & Mersey Canal. Turn right to descend to the canal towpath and follow it forward to another bridge, where you climb up to the road.

An alternative route at this point is not to climb to the road but to continue along the towpath. Eventually you come to Derwentmouth Lock, which, as its name indicates, is close to the mouth of the River Derwent, the point you were looking at earlier from across the Trent.

Cross the canal by the lock gates (this is quite legal, but care should be exercised – not suitable for most dogs), and locate a footpath passing through the small wood behind the lock.

Follow this footpath which crosses a large field to a stile close by the bank of the River Derwent. Follow this path left through several fields alongside the Derwent, upstream to a footbridge over the river, here converging with the main walk.

On your left are two canalside public houses, the New Inn and the Malt Shovel, in case you feel in need of refreshment at this half-way point. Otherwise continue the walk forward over the bridge and along the road, which has little traffic. This takes you out of Shardlow to the hamlet of Great Wilne which has a number of attractive dwellings. At the end of the road, climb the stile, and cross the field diagonally to the footbridge you can see ahead.

Cross the footbridge, and at the lane turn right and follow it back to Sawley, passing over the M1 motorway into Wilne Road.

ST CHAD'S WATER

The walk around the lake is about one mile and is suitable for wheelchair users. You can either follow the above instructions in reverse from Sawley to Church Wilne for a longer walk, or drive to the car park opposite Wilne Church for the shorter option.

The hamlet of Church Wilne was once a dependency of Sawley. However, most of the population moved to Draycott, ¾ mile away, leaving the magnificent church in an isolated position. Opposite the church is a nature reserve formed round a lake known as St Chad's Water, itself created from gravel workings of which there have been many around Sawley. A walk round the lake is always a pleasant stroll, particularly for bird lovers.

Approximately 100 yards south of Church Wilne, next to the river Derwent, is Wilne Mill, the site of the ancient watermill probably mentioned in Domesday. The current building is occupied by a factory, formerly making fireworks but now producing explosives.